THE WANTED

THE WANTED

michael tyrell

The National Poetry Review Press
Aptos, California

The National Poetry Review Press
(an imprint of DHP)
Post Office Box 2080, Aptos, California 95001-2080

Printed in the United States of America
Published in 2012 by The National Poetry Review Press

ISBN 978-1-935716-17-4

Cover artwork:

The Bank Executives
Finger painted on an iPhone 2g
by Matthew Watkins
www.watkinsmedia.com

For the Three Elizabeths

TABLE OF CONTENTS

In the morning I walked to the bank. I went to the automated teller machine to check my balance. I inserted my card, entered my secret code, tapped out my request. The figure on the screen roughly corresponded to my independent estimate. . . The system had blessed my life. I felt its support and approval. The system hardware, the mainframe sitting in a locked room in some distant city. What a pleasing interaction. I sensed that something of deep personal value, but not money, not that at all, had been authenticated and confirmed...The system was invisible, which made it all the more impressive, all the more disquieting to deal with. But we were in accord, at least for now. The networks, the circuits, the streams, the harmonies.

—Don DeLillo, *White Noise*

He looked toward the window and the face there seemed to suggest that he might be inadequate to the day's exactions. He wondered if he would even recognize the city when they came to it.

—Flannery O'Connor, *A Good Man Is Hard to Find*

I was a solid among other solids.

—Samuel Beckett, *Molloy*

I.

INVISIBLE STATION

In tunnels now you try to put them together every
uniform every coin you watch the stations black out
the police composite in every stop not one but
more than one uniform in this car more than one you
every face in the black glass a coin in a stopped fountain
signs for emergency and the brake in reach should they pull it
the tunnel every instant a blackout should you stop it
even in daylight they couldn't read the platform's faces
even if they stopped they could never move again they must dart
below streets where walkers stumble move closer
into compartments into elevators a door can make anything
vanish in this instant a child falling into a well can hear
echoes talk back to her the world contracts to a blue
circle she can't hear a train or a voice only birds
filling in the circle and the tapping of her watch she hasn't stopped
someone is calling her and the silence follows her name
the wrong response follows it the bell of the train-door
opening and someone getting out and someone getting on
name of place your name my name zero plus zero plus zero

THE WANTED

Never been wanted
like the ones in the government posters, never
been pegged in the bureaus of authority

as unapprehended,
all my arsons day-dreamed,
such-and-such heart left thumping always

in the cage where I found it,
every alibi, if not airtight,
then spit-sealed in an envelope

in which words will sting,
not explode, and only if read.
Never been like the servants who think they're bosses,

kept safe by bulletproof glass,
as if they too are wanted—their smiles and
scars on view, like those on the loose.

Never can remember
when they were separate—
my face and my name, when want only meant lack

and want meant only wanting, when I believed
wanting nothing
would keep me from vanishing.

PUBLIC PHONE

And on the receiver's live air, the insistent hello
from someone who has refused to hang up, the plea
divorced from all name or form,
an argument's last word splintering
through the black pinpoints,
warped as the metal where the dialer's face floated
above square numbers, where
every voice is listed under code, like combinations
to an immense vault of wires.
Only static has figured all of them out.
I hear it like a safecracker's tools thieving through connection,
if being invisible can be called connection.
Now it is silencing my answers
to the other voice, the living one.
Now it is peeling the two wires apart.
Has it decoded even the walkers
whose garments brush against the window glass?
I can hear their voices only in fragments,
like taped voices being rewound and then deleted.
The shopping-center doors clap shut and open,
the atonal hum returns, and out there, unidentifiable
in the crowds, how decisively the dialer must still be moving,
propelling himself from the argument,
forgetting, by degrees, the voice, the face, the number.
How decisively he's abandoning them—
murmuring *it's not impossible, really,*
nothing can reach me as the poles
follow him, faceless totems surrounding
and claiming every imaginable distance.

THE BYSTANDER

Hoarder of clues, the eye lives apart
from the brain's emergency advice—

feral, trained to tail the unknown
skirt and coat through the revolving door's mirrors,

alert to her destination, that window
she'll step from to reach her standstill, her very own ledge.

I have hands and no heart for alarms.
Don't ask for evidence, I'm the exit.

Only the pickpocket's features burn,
unforgettable, in my sights. In stairwells

I'll hide from the looters,
the lit ashcan's open, apocalyptic eye.

Anyone recorded is mortal: when the hunter
startles Diana in the water, amnesia divides his pack,

they find him by his new howl.
I know the false witnesses—the headline's defining smear,

the onlookers' chanted *jump, jump, jump*.
Rescue, elaborate harm—I feel no distinction.

AGORA

The woman on cable television pinches a bullet....
oh that collision, that near-miss you just swerved from,
going where you went....that Never Again....

What you won't do. And whom.
Look, this hovel can be a kind of cold storage—
not farmed out, you can't atrophy.

But craving for the latest accolade
propels you to a contest
where the tunic has to be worn just so.

The eminent surrogates make their cuts quickly.
Next in line: placebo groups,
lobotomized wolves. Something will adopt you—

Will you keep it, will the devouring woods permit you?
A body becomes a needle
in such undirected space: to stick things or lose itself.

When the place-names squeal
on their hinges, you notice no one's about
to oil them, and all these novel accessories

stand for ancient souvenirs you've so
heartlessly replaced. You're alone
by pure coincidence, or coincidence

momentarily makes you un-alone—
a chain letter bears a familiar ambergris,
in the wreckage you grab a hand you recognize.

SUPERSTITION, INC.

So I lose track. Galoshes dry on my table.
Do I court sorrow by bringing old brooms into a new house?

I'm just learning not to walk under ladders
when the mirrors (meant to expand space) go to smithereens.

The notice, the seven-year bitch, arrives in the mail.
I want a reprieve, but the voice menu of Superstition Inc. starves me.

I'm sorry, I don't understand
the omen you just entered.

The letters on the annual eye-chart grow dimmer.
I touch the orbits, the future hollows, there's something to this—

Belief has been part of my treatment,
a game of love and love-not until

a brittle stem, my person, remains.
Like the semester's dissections, all sutured.

An incantation a movie taught me—
a synonym for stupid or beautiful or miracle.

A messenger slides his invitations
under my door. Every day, he would bring

calligraphy, the psychic inkings, leaves
lashed to the vacant transom, my corner of peril

where like the myopic streetwalker
I rush to kiss whatever luck shows up.

X-RAY VISION

In the first decade
I was sure I was from Krypton—
look at me now, losing my voice
at a booth called Information,
a directory speculating
every name of the man
who seized your firstborn.
Is he the one loading a rifle
in the second-story window,
veering a circle right into Information?
His curtain the American emblem,
only a silhouette like a puppet
comes through, plus this laser beam,
electronic Eucharist on our
foreheads. We are the designated
victims, and the woman walking
the empty leash applauds
his good taste. In releasing
updates it seems we have
become rumors ourselves.
I have cried wolf so many times
I expect the authorities
will start crank-calling me.
Hours are the Kryptonite,
can't count how many go skyward.
There is no time
allotted for transformation.
The man with the rifle sends his love.

MARKETPLACE

For a downtown plaza,
for a clue to the shell game,
for wind
that takes me for a tree that does not move,
I give you silver, I give you a killed balloon,
I give you ruined film.

For a whore,
for a tongue of my own,
I give you the vacant glove.
For a train, for a toy wall,
for a wooden fish, for a chaperon.

I give you a mask fit for surgery.
For the syllable.
For the kernel
under the shell.
For my mouth
that takes my mask
for some other mouth.

THE BOOKS

I'm looking for the characters who got away,
because even the books aren't behaving themselves
these days—
the pages blank, every page, I keep losing my place,
hero foil archenemy static dynamic—I'm looking for the ones
who got away, got the money,
ran away with Quilty, went to Thornfield
and burned it up, and something I'm supposed
to remember about redemption,
the firemen who knew the temperature at which books burn,
the thought criminals of the year we passed decades ago.
Redemption, who did they kill for it—
the carver of soap dolls in Maycomb,
the one I met once, the one I never saw again,
the one in Hollywood who sold her body
so Vaudeville Harry could have a funeral?
Where did they end up,
how did they get out of the pages,
that man and woman in the gazebo
outside my window,
did they burn themselves out?
Did they come from all the books in the future
in flames set by the firemen,
or were they the ones who resisted,
who read the books long enough
to *become* the books—
I could do this, I could read
all the blank pages around me,
if only I wasn't tired of fiction,
almost cold enough to believe
a fire will do me better.

II.

IT HAS BEEN WEEKS SINCE THE CARNIVAL

In the morning the children
steal the clothes, put them in trees.
All the furs, overalls, the underthings,
the heretics and penitents, the whole town
plucked from a line where it doesn't *know*
it's waiting, all the king's horses and men.
There is less of the sky now,
its whore's eye-shadow,
fewer buyers, the clouds capillary-thin.
It's sealed up, the view of the factory
we recently suspected was our destination all along,
a trip where the point seemed not to pack.
Branches are spokes, are not apertures
that each seem to compete for a sliver of heaven,
or a heaven only satin and sequin over the empty thing.
Branches are not doors but why are there keys,
twisted as if tried,
rusting in drains. Without leaves, we saw more of the sky.
Clothes behave like flowers, they attract mouths.
The children nudge, stuck in tunnels under the street.
The children lock themselves in tinted cars.
They balance on fire escapes and tiptoe on scaffolding.
They are within walking distance of the great tragedy.
They will not come down for all the pearls on the bridge.
The mothers have fallen asleep looking for pencils.
The fathers have fallen asleep at a movie about oranges.
How many years have passed like this, among statues
we didn't commission. We need the correct joke,
a deed or notarized license, a simultaneous
interpreter for our delays and quiets and paroxysms.
In the morning the moon is no coin,
we have to make do with these solitudes
that seem added to like savings accounts and these
leaves we stick on our bodies like the original pair, but
where to put such difficult children
who do not cry or tumble when we want them to.
They make themselves immune to sugar;
the ponies will not lure them down.
It has been weeks since the carnival, remember

how unmoving the moving target was,
how brilliantly painted the carousel,
better to think of those horses than these,
the oils and cranks we never saw
that kept them galloping,
and we could watch and watch and watch
because we were not the ones who rode them.

HANDLE AND BLADE

Forcing seed into noncommittal soil
I come across an old knife
minus handle, hooked blade gone orange
with once-rain or once-blood.

Upside down it becomes a question
next to exhumed roots and stones,
weapon without victim,
tool of no particular use.
Rust tastes like iron,

like blood sucked in from a cut:
anything ruined tastes like that,
though the openings
come together, sometimes
sealed by color. All day
I poke in seeds almost sure to fail.
Blood under fingernails,
specked with earth, pinned with thorns.

In sun the knife can't glint,
its smile dulled under years: if only
I could locate the handle, grip
the end broken in front of me—
were it thrust into some famous corpse,
would a museum want it?

The earth is fragment and glass,
the earth is smoothed over,
seeds no longer visible,
flies lighting on the rusted knife.
They know things I don't:
keep moving,
keep to the surfaces—
the body, the rusted invention.

THE LOVERS IN THE LIFEGUARD CHAIR

I'm not the first frustrated astronomer
staring farther than my corrected vision
can take me. Love not mine is better
than none. Two friends I can't save for a tryst
join me at the border where the tides
hiss, and our heckling initially makes sense,
three craning necks, what's the couple
up to, who's on top, who will break free first.
See who seems to steer the narrow bars
holding up the stalled prow good enough for borrowing.
Then it's our envy we see sharper than our pleasure—
as in the movies, we don't get to choose
the ending or topple the lovely when we want.
Like tenants emerging from a still-smoldering
building, clutching the rungs in reverse,
they come down to sand, these two—it rescues them
from falling backward; they brush off
their torn-wing garments in the capsule of light
that restores them to feature and color.
And not one of us will admit we've never done
anything that vulnerable.

SECOND LANGUAGE

Hello, goodbye, I don't want it.
City of warped steps spawning markets

where muslin is scissored to tamp the mouth
against illness, against words.

Third stop, exit stubs, passport mugshots in hand.
Fur hats that fall apart. Pockets with fissures.

Help me, what's the word for *not enough hands.*
What's the word for: not one *hello* from one face behind

the tables, not one *goodbye* nor a single first name

learned from the coal-burning trains.

Bones endure longer. Sockets fit
(not frame) this background,

the Great Wall like glittering cartilage,
night made from coal dust whistling the open parts.

Builders are buried here. Unknown.
That much can be counted on.

And the vendor's last best offer—
branches of candied haw, souvenir bones—

bone over branch over stub over passport
we must accept, we have to,
city not yours, not mine—

to build a way over.

Need your immediate input on this.
Need you to put yourself out, go the last mile.
Our bases must touch on the double.
Actually, you don't look well at all.
Take this expired painkiller and write your symptoms on it.

Back to our initiative like I was saying.
Do you know what a dust particle is?
I had you collate some, oh a million or so, once.
Do you know what a camera is?
I used mine to copy you so you wouldn't pilfer.

This is a shrink ray. I'm the me in team.
You'll inhabit this slide, this atomic cubicle.
Come to think of the gushing bacteria as everyday traffic.
We've already faxed your emergency contacts.
This is the experiment, this is the rumor in the mill.

We've assigned your caseload
to the next best inferior.
It's paid vacation. It's bigger than Sputnik.
You'll be the noble proof, I'll hypothesize.
We might complete the enlargement beam in time.

But if not, we've reserved the smallest conceivable
urn, adjacent to the power source.
First these two scratched marbles peering at me.
You'll scare less if you can't look in the mirror before you go.
Do it for those young caroling ones you see outside.

It's like their playground, that swatch of sky on the upswing.
See. Saw. Am. Was.

THE SUPPORTING CHARACTER

The narration's unreliable.
Cowering before the French doors,
I arrange myself with the props.
Any minute now, the sofa
could become an executioner's chair.
There's evidence of foreshadowing
everywhere: scribbled entries,
a messenger with news of arson,
a postcard from Babylon.
At the intersection between
altar and aisle, the bodiless gown.
The guests can't get in.
They are cursing and pounding at stained glass.
For me there is no deviation,
no madwoman in the attic.
I'm a subplot about to unfold,
others will be written out before I bellow
my first words. Where will I be mentioned,
and how—as inbred brother, lascivious killer?
I pray for more decades, as if
a conflict could embrace me,
a bildungsroman, but already the deterministic
lines are scanning the scene,
only the landscape will be described.

The desert of the one country that will soon be another,
        and the seven (women, men) entering a third
(no, fourth) day on foot, and nightfall, and hatching
            (no, don't say it) things that can't cross

traintracks. What country are they in when they fold in
        half upon the trains (is this their pose) and in one
country that will soon be another, these mechanisms
        I call mine, two eyes, are boring into a landscape

of trees (the body leaves the soul I am told) and the trees
        look to be human, their shapes are lying. In
Egon Schiele's painting, which is the body, which the landscape?
        These hands (who said they were mine) could no more raise

the sleepers from the tracks than this country become another.
        Schiele looked at himself, tore out the human, cleaved
it into branches. The soul begins by finding the pieces, assembling
        them into trees that look over traintracks, desert trees.

I can't find the human in them (would I want to), nor
        can they return what I see. Entering dayfall and nightfall
on foot, how they must feel, of course they know trains
        don't run at night in Mexico. Once, to prove a point,

I lay down on tracks (this was my friends' pose) as
        the minutes of nightfall hurried to make me part
of their landscape, they were painting me iron-color, almost asleep
        and the train would paint me too. The body leaves

the soul I am told. They are finding sleep, the seven
        lying down, nothing can't be retracted or revised,
they are in one piece and in the morning I will find them here,
        Schiele in his grave, the train out of one country

hurrying into another.

THE BRIDLE

What use is grief to a horse?
—Peter Shaffer, *Equus*

Because the husband was dead,
I could ride his horse.
Because the widow handed me the bridle
and five singles. Because hoofbeats
could cloud the mustard road,
the earth rose when I rode in circles.
The children appeared where I could see them,
the wife told me they were childless.
I was childless, a child because this
was not my second ride. The children
knew about dreams and surrounded me
as if they wanted something, crouching
on the roadside boulders. Do children
have to exist in order to disappear?
They wanted something: not the rider.
Not the earth. They crept out.
They crouched where I could see them.
Their faces touched each other like magnets.
It was New Year's Eve
and the horse wanted rest, the skeleton
buried under the hide, under the horse.
It was between the wife
and husband. The earth wanted the horse,
wanted all of us childless. Because we could
dream of disappearing. Because the earth
would dream of us, now we would disappear.

AGAINST ANGELS

In the stained glass of St. Anthony's church,
they flew too perfectly, arriving everywhere,
like guests who never decline invitation,
outlasting their welcome, gossips
in gardens, mangers, temples, at any eventful site
where their golden wings would be
superfluous, and Lucifer's example
the notable absence, the reminder
how paradise gets lost every day on earth.
Named for the archangel, each Sunday
I walked under the raised swords
of the seraphs and wondered what bribery,
what innocence could earn the blond hair
and blinding haloes ascending to countries of clouds,
what barter to molt my body
and again touch the body of my father?

The legends of Joan and Sebastian,
the priest insisted: feathers shot from their shoulders,
each became identical,
not in size but character, no true sex,
none desiring touch or favoring
silence over music. And, as I hunted the ceiling
for a proof of their human lives, I found
nothing, not a single arrow, I saw each hovering god
no different than the stone-faced images
guarding local graves, their open hands
not a welcome into light
but a gesture of dismissal,
a rejection of the body that stood against
the wings on those windows,
and the iron bars behind them.

THE DARE

The dog is fenced-in. The dog is playing wolf in our time.
The neighbor shears all season, his yard a bride.
Penalty is edible. The wolf is eating gunpowder.
I marry my cousin. The woods are made of cells
like a hive. The houses change color. The dog
is drooling to eat one of us. The dare is to go in.
They are naming the town a harbor.
The husband is pulling the woodbine
and the woodbine grows. The roots and cells
have wills of their own. You are playing Hide.
One of us is bleeding. One of us is eating.
The house has splintery boards for doors.
The neighbor can see us through shears.
His grass is blazed by woodbine. He snips
up everything yellow. My cousin uses chalk
to make a house. The boards and doors
stand open. I am one of the spies. To prove
you were there, you take what you can.
The dare is to get out. The marriage vow
is made in the woods. The woodbine is meant
to be eaten. Our house is empty, our house is rented.
Our game is our dare. The houses are pulling
up the old houses. The shears can see us.
I am standing in the empty house.
Fireworks are gunpowder. The dog won't survive.
You say the town is empty. The town is a hive.
To prove I was there, I take a bride.

III.

The mewling carrier of plague fixed to the glue strip,
like the accused it had the right.
And the recidivist in the elevator,

his point well-made, an Exacto to my throat.
He spoke anyway. He had the right.
Tonight, the trees should keep their anthropomorphized

opinions to themselves, the parked fuck-cars should
rust unopened. No loitering: We should follow the sign's advice.
But we have the right to be here.

I envy the figures in flop plays, their sorry dialogue.
We live on pauses,
the gun fires blanks in the last act.

My name will become meaningful
after you count it off nine-hundred
ninety-nine, ninety-eight times, like a beer on the wall—

In the business of the auction
the thing on the block must
get sold, sound or unsound—

do I not hear
one thousand—say it to my face—
this face that can't launch one thousand.

OCTOBER IN IDLEVILLE

O love, my has-been, I've heard the huddled cheerleaders
planning a kamikaze mission, they want
the crowd to suffer a gorgeous terror,
like last night, mailboxes overturned by the Visiting Team,
they don't want morning and order to come,
Jupiter Electronics hesitantly kick-standing its doors—
I think I'm like the floor model monitors on display,
all on the Accu-weather channel,
translating everything into Arctic,
World's Best Avalanches,
Come and Knock on Our Igloo,
no wonder so little business today,
who but me wants winter before they deserve.
Winter means our reunion, my harlequin,
you're not a has-been
but an about-to-be, and we'll be hemispheres from the stadium.
O City that pollutes its way out of seasons and blindfolds stars!
I'll have to guess which squad car you're hiding behind.
Finding you allows me to be the cop, the doctor, and the
    schoolmaster.
And no Cassandra from out of her Secrets of the Future $5
    storefront
strangling my forearm to warn me
this is the wrong love, this will be slow to end,
the mosaic made to slice the admiring fingers,
fingers which must assimilate each tessera,
done in all the colors of foliage the Idleville husbands pour
illegally into the derelict yards—
You are like them, the leaves.
You should arrive with the disclaimer tag,
I am easy to rip off & take x.5 years to dissolve

Puppet, my mouthpiece, my spineless shadow,
what have I buried and where? I thought when
it was dark I could find it in the garden,
but the earth there was as vacant as you, who won't
dance or contradict unless a hand is buried in you.
I could drown you a thousand nights
and still you'd come back to me without a soul.

Unlike this house, its three souls: all women.
I am alive, I don't understand how they can sleep.
The garden flowers are an audience of trembles.
Tiger lilies tilt, their lips sealed as vipers.
I've always liked walking at night, not dreaming.
Indoors I pace like Hansel in the witch's cell,
holding up bones for the night trees that watch me.

You are not like them, my puppet. Your eyes
roll shut when I drop you to the ground.
You can't hear the living, their icy demands.
Even now their hands are closing on something,
the bedsheet or the moon.
Turning, crying out.
There is no one else in the room.

False summer, clients unwinding their bandages,
shadows anchoring the shoes.

Most unlucky to be loved, the diviner murmurs.
A man carries his future in a
saucer's elliptical groove.

Glass of the storefronts blurs
whatever passes, can only hold what can't move,
or can't move too far—
the offices, the city tree, the city tree's branches.

The man with the stroller
is pointing out the child's form in the glass,
to step away from recognition
is to step toward the world.

See how the branches make a signature,
an unrecognizable form? The child
considers this being that exists apart from it—

how does it know the next move exactly,
seems to know the future and the child's room?

Knows even fire touching a sleeve,
fingers moving in panic.
Lucky to be unloved,
how the leaves hold on to us in the glass, our fortunes.

We hold on to what can harm us.

DECADE: NEW YORK

O dollars I let fly from the moon-roof.
Blindfolds that launched from the dogwood,
I thought you meant I was kidnapped

because ten times I was blinded and ten times I lost you.
Did hands perform this countdown?
I felt pinned, bare page under paperweight

while voices recited the secret texts,
like nets that lose the most valuable.
I could have *been* somebody.

Let my follicles push their tips to earth,
taught the soles of my feet to tolerate fire.
Someone devastating fled up a hail-stoned stoop

and left the door ajar, glanced my way.
I could have come into that kingdom, come undone,
come into a fortune enough to choke a fountain.

Goods I shed to lead me in
until the labyrinth became obvious, maybe never was.
I threw away Orpheus, or tuned him out.

Burned my rival's poems,
as if this would transform me.
If I were a street I would have accepted

Godzilla's claw by now, resurrected
my wicked venues, given back
a sneezing child from the cistern.

Against my will, I would have severed
just as the lovers begged opposite.
A boulevard can survive its iniquities,

A map doesn't talk back like a calendar.
You wouldn't approach me as one human to another.
You wouldn't take my clothes off in the same way.

STRANGER WITHOUT CANDY

do I know it yet the first law of shadow where
the gesture is larger than the body of the one who produces it
the playground stranger a Goliath who can still fit in the curved saddle

of the oiled swing   he lingers he does not swing doesn't kick
the eye's enemy the pebbled dust where the a.m. visitors like me
conduct their chanting interring cicada and Batman

they carve the score me vs. you in imported sand
entirely disowned by the sea and sure enough he's saying now
come here   he's not a father perhaps he someone's son

he's every foul love we ever coveted closed kiss stinging
of red vinegar one hand chaperoned behind his back and
barriers all around him a fence of spears and above telescopes

aimed from windows of the stacked apartments and between
the padlock the permission he's dangling the passkey in the
hand he's calling me with   Hold out your hand he says

not such a complicated story there still it erodes every day
wise will make a grave wise will dig a lover's bed in years to come
listen do I know there are places where shadows don't count

I float I'm the first astronaut off the ship there is nowhere
not to get to   the air is borrowed I like it   I was a child
only I can tell you   only the escape outlives the monument

SELF-PORTRAIT THROUGH ELECTRIC EYE

he exists without hunger he can never be apprehended
he stepped over the sensors his frame
a lie detector a forgery Lost and Found where only
a crime can find you how the evidence accumulates
in the schoolyard each morning the blind child
learns shape learns outline and I avoid his hands
a more powerful species of seeing   am I wrong
once they erased me by just letting me go
I thought invisibility was enough losing my uniform
no you must squeeze past him I tell myself
he can hear you breathing you won't let him read you
you must learn to be nothing that trembles

I WILL BE YOUR CUSTOMER THIS EVENING

No tintype or snapshot to compare myself
with the dressed-to-the-nines, all-thumbs waiter
at sixes-and-sevens, who made me
23 chromosomes what I am
but whom I've never met,
only this pronounced brow and jaw line,
my meager alleged inheritance
I magnify each morning,
this likeness on its squeaky accordion
I pull forward and hone raw
to keep the paychecks coming,
to deny glances of sympathy on the street.
I'm like a street of my own
I have to wander and raze
until I get to the end of this face
and reach marble corridor, gilded sconces,
a dining room, a table of vulgar apostles
who can't spare a napkin for a shaving cut.
The server I'm heir to gets curses
and laughable tips but refuses to quit, he's
Rasputin as much I'm the hemophiliac
prince without a title.
At my table I'm in my war paint
but who the hell at my table wants to talk war,
they've done that before, been there,
all they want is ice for their phantom limbs.
I need an ingredient viler than a fly
in my soup,
a fishbone to asphyxiate on,
a tip better than cash to lure him over.
How will I call him if he answers?
I have no idea what he answers to.
We've never been properly introduced,
my servant, my sponsor, and he's
no garçon, no Hey Bub, Daddy-O.
Whistles are for mutts, my fingers too shaky for snaps.
The charitable gluttons throw me
a few wafers, no body of Christ
but host is the only word I can think of,

host is the farthest from what I am,
host is what I will say when I see him,
host sounds best.

IV.

THE SURROGATE

*Luminol: a chemical sprayed at crime
scenes, making blood glow.*

Results squeak by in their white loafers.
They are not mine yet,
not yours.
I'm as illiterate as the undelivered,
the magazine paragraphs turned skyscrapers

studied from a squinting distance—
and this shield I was counting on

(prayer is more counting than prayer now)

dissolves with the other appetites
because I must be tested first,

and before I'm a donor
I'm first and necessarily a loiterer,

and up to this point I've been fortunate
and shrewd enough not to smile in photographs
because only victims smile, everyone knows that,

or at least the people in this room auditioning
for a future abide by it, every mouth a machine
that will not be switched on.
The mother
across the room putting a finger to her lips,
and her little girl locking up her voice
with the pretend key, tosses the key down.

No hope of shutting up the desk attendant's radio.

Updates from the world: be happy you're in here,
where every drop's held until the last possible moment.

I know it should console me that we can't
erase it, that the offense can be read
by the light it gives, a prosaic intensity,

decorative stars tacked to a tenement ceiling.

The turning point's pointless
suspense demands from every surrounding
a significant clue. I should know.

I won't remember my old zip codes, I won't remember
the name of the surrogate who picked me up from school
the day my mother walked in on a burglar

and now I feel no proof: that my mother
made it out in one piece, my mother

escaped the burglar and I, my mother—

I know it should almost console me.

I thought by now I'd be the easy believer,
not the investigator
with no wish for the terrible to be undone,

Only tell me *how* it was done—

THREE TICKETS TO THE LOTTERY

1. January Potluck

germs of endearment—fusion soup—no wine—
I am an unknown—a ghost-guest—I get confidences—
when they first met—who went into rehab first—host or the missus—

all things needed to puncture a wall—how to
make a contrived *there*—pole in the center like a topless bar—
where they broke past to make this room belonging

to the sun—are we outside or inside now—
walls and conversation collapsible—chuckles not laughter—
"When I was in Germany I saw such goats and took their pictures"—

they have a mattress here that remembers the
sleeper—what marriage must accomplish—
bed no longer capable of amnesia—

bed recording interlopers—jetlagged lady who
drowses there—she saw the best hospital in Vienna—
I would not be here without her—

I flubbed the coordinates—the house number—
the wrong voice on the intercom telling me
I was wrong—an editor of destinations—

what luck I brought here was not food—
when does the year stop being New—
when do we stop saying it—

twelve violet tulips in the vase—twelve
I brought—next to the race on the screen—
no one pays attention to—someone has to win—

2. Mother

She quits playing her i.q., my birthday—
They don't make money—

in the little stadium of the living room—

The television man following the ball's trajectory—
she registering the correct discouragement from the couch
where she later tries sleep—the phone out—no machine—

She is standing at the baggage claim in heaven—
the correct valise the one with the baby inside.
She should take everything but doesn't—

In such lotteries a good baby makes it difficult—
I hate it none of them could be me, my crying always relentless—
that interval of life when a life seems most random—

what you have to get through to get to any life—
new or otherwise— I am no mathematician—
I still cling to horoscopes—

I can speak of nothing else—how many
I have to pay back—
when mine will be up— how much a new son for her would cost—

I could *do* a number but she never cared for my voice—
She had other equations to figure out—
I thought "meet" was edible in "make ends meet"—

even the music judge never convinced her—
not the praise he wrote—
not the perfect score—

3. Manic Panic

defines me, desperate to be incognito—
if I cannot prevent coincidental sightings of you
I'll revise how I'm sighted—

bifocals—fat-suit—surgically reduced limbs—
I buy a bottle of Manic Panic hair dye—Hydrant Red—
when I see you traversing Eighth Street—

where they say the first baseball was played—
which is not code for some initial undressing—

at least we used codes then—I've never—where now—

your phony lovely blondness electrical—like Angelica Huston
in *The Grifters*—compare the whole thing
to laughing at a joke you don't get—

scratch that—as I should trade Hydrant
for something waterless—please, no metaphors for weeping—
like falling for a grift—the "act of faith" costs dearly—

I'd have something missing—lineup on the calculator
short of Infinity—if we only had a project—
now an epitaph—an entry in the International Star Registry—

we are open to coincidence by geography—
you are still wearing your gold—
I still have my life savings—

THE CHAIRMAN'S COFFIN

Arctic as an aquarium the casket glass—
Mao's face warping in overhead light, hair greased
back like a crooner's, the eyes stitched or glued.

I miss my camera, the shutter's neutral
absolutes: negatives or amnesia.
A place air never enters, like memory.

How negotiable a body: a souvenir,
a mausoleum—disownable as the personal effects
monitored by entrance guards.

No second looks, says the timer,
pulse in a pocket of the guide.
My hand is stamped with blue permissions,

my ice-caked shoes following peers to the public square.
Can sharks stop even once?
There's a price for breathing. A bullet's not free.

DESERT: INSOMNIA

Often you carry its wrinkles
into daylight, where the sleepers recommend
yoga or warm milk, good sex to make
the body drowsy. They look funny
when you announce that you've named
every crack in your ceiling. What do they know?
They spent all their lives dreaming,
gone maybe once to the lifelong school you've
attended, the windowless classroom
with yourself as the only student.
Boredom teaches nothing but endurance.
No one ever hires a teacher, and you spend
all your time at arithmetic, counting alarm-
clock hours, measuring loss as the geniuses snore
in softer rooms. And you think of the moonish
faces that leaned over your crib,
which parent gave you this gene? There's no
trace, no one to blame because the pills stopped
working, no way to track this river to its source.
The geography of bedtime is immense,
but so what? You still float and float
as in a canoe without paddles,
sleep drifts farther away from your clutches.
You think this is how they'll find you
after mourners have watched last breaths,
when paramedics have wrapped your feet,
and you, open-eyed, still wondering
why you never thought of this before.

NIGHT SWIMMER

Among the shore's washed-up warnings—
the shattered nautilus, the floating
luggage of the dead—you move
to a territory blacker than the places
we touched: step into it, if you must,
let the undertow latch your nude ankles.
I knew the fire would not keep you;
you'd rather walk blindly than hold still.
So strip without threat of sunburn,
vandalize the dunes with your limbs.
It's time to enter the wet bladed edges
which break us again into separate beings,
pour salt into wherever we bleed.

V.

EXIT WOUND

He wanted a cave. Spoke back to vices out of the alley, where hummers and hearses flashed like a toy gun's blanks. Coats he lent to children raised by wolves. In a classroom, the uniforms asked him to write his name over and over. Then he auctioned his wife. He wanted a cave they gave him a cell. He wanted zeroes. He willed his eyes at the DMV to the not-yet-blind. He owed apologies, coins, binoculars, a bridle for the horse that outlived its owners. He ate salt only. He painted mannequins they became his kin. He shot three he shot four where were the ghosts? He sat with the author and tried on his FITS ALL. He sleeptalked. They fed him capsules. They gave him the author and the author's capsules. They offered him paper he bled a few words out of it. He skipped 3 life sentences. They read him, the fugitive Braille of his stunted limbs. They called to him. He lost his voice. He broke himself in two. They brought him back to life.

I never pick flowers anymore, and these weak buds
are no exception. I didn't choose them; so can I feign
they chose me, somehow grew exactly under the bench
I sat on, delaying my walk toward Brown Street,
offerings scarcely better than the limp-necked dandelions
I carried in childhood to the mother of God.
I wanted no reminders, no guaranteed handful
of the past. Yet, sitting there, I couldn't stop thinking how
even weeds once stood for intercession; as though
all roots could connect, carry voices back,
even the joking nicknames I knew them by,
and the seeds I scattered that never grew
meant, however briefly, I had punched through.
And now my palms marked by what—blood
or chlorophyll sounds equally wrong.
How can you refuse what you can't name?
Even though they're less vivid than mortuary flowers,
these bring me to the foot of stones
I see in dreams but cannot reach, walking among names
no longer legible, grown beyond grasp.

THE SUITORS

Victim, Crossing, Child and Mother,
everywhere I walk. Armature, outline.
Match-black *instructions*, the bit players we call *strangers.*
Everywhere I walk, I size them up,
details toxic in their permanence.
The missing girl's poster.
Have you heard what the missing girl's mother sees
seventeen years later?
She's not thirty-four, she's seventeen.
I see her on the screen when the power's turned off.
Without a blackout, can a story complete its listener?
And without them noticing, I eavesdrop on
everyone around me. Are they in your custody, Recollection,
these voices that hypnotize?
They must be answered first, they must be made to answer me.
And where in the cave-dark of the alley is the story
complete, are the echoes a form of punishment?
End of summer, every night
of summer, exterior clamoring through the window,
I watch the shore, listening to my mother
the murmuring inventor,
her threads unwinding, ceaselessly noosing their closures
so far from everywhere I wander.
Sometimes she takes a break.
Hands weaving in fear of extinction.
Am I one of the automatons, one of her suitors?
Will this be my only island,
with its ballad tide that never finishes?
And the father, the father who could step into any frame,
did he exist in the first place, can he touch me?
If the threads stop, I know our lives could stop.
I stare out among conspirators as if through brood cells,
counting my turn to be stung, to sting.
On the shore, the dancing figures, the optimists.
If nothing can disappear, where do their fires go?
If the tide is not fire, why does it flicker?

ORPHEUS AT LETHE

And at the river's mouth, the end of memory.
I could make you remember: deaf Charon,

how the oars gleam when she crosses
as a shadow,
able to be led in any direction.

Why is tonight any different—
you rushing back into the grotto,
thrusting forward against the dream,

cupping that black water in both hands,
your mouth open, your eyes
altered when you look up, ruined—

My eyes open: I'm alone in the bed.

The blinds are raised, the street lamps
emptying streaks of dull gold
into the room. Night isn't finished—

you can't flee back to the outside world yet.
So you stand here facing the framed tenements,
the bands of strangers busy getting lost.

Two years. Still you won't speak
the name, turning instead to your mirrors:
they duplicate anything,
they will always keep you company.

If you came to me now, would you
see yourself passing through them?

Look: I could make you remember—
she is nowhere in this room.

What is the future but more memory?

NIGHT STATIONS

You stand in the coldest night of the year,
only a ticket for company.

How frozen the town below looks:
the boarded-up Baptist church, the parked cars
iced to their hoods.
And now the moon, which signifies nothing—

In the future, the train will be late too, as it is now;
absence will precede it, a kind of messenger—

Who will occupy the row of iron seats
where that shivering couple sit, too hypothermic to embrace?
The others will depart before you get here.

Alone over the dark tracks,
you'll be spying the tunnel for the headlamp's spark—
pray for one more.

No belongings on either side,
nothing to be stolen, not even a glove.
That's how you tell
a passenger has no one to meet—

one numb evening, the planks nailed in place.
And wind flipping a ticket
where the stops are written.

DO NOT DUPLICATE

The train's armor shudders and stops.
Too nearsighted to see ghosts,
I'm too old to name the other riders.

I hesitate before metal detectors
in stores where I haven't stolen.
The tongue-tied clerk eyes me

like the voice teacher who ordered me
to hold breaths 10, 20 beats.
I don't remember the penalty;

I still second-guess safe landings,
duck snapshots and group poses.
Out-of-towners ask me directions in public parks.

I take another man's wife,
clothing, live reptiles. I open the family
album and no one recognizes me.

A cop berates a woman in nun's
clothing as I cross the Avenue of the Americas.
Coins rattle in her black sleeves.

My boss's keys say *Do Not Duplicate.*
I remember phone numbers I shouldn't remember.
A hornet landed on my tongue once, then lifted away.

FAMILY UNDERWORLD

1. Indian Summer

She postpones the return trip, detained
by her mother's abundance,
her insistence: keep the trees one color.

Afterimage, some nights
she is visible to him
emerging from incorruptible stone.

That he has a kingdom to play with
means little to him.
He sees obedient captives,
vessels waiting to be poured and tossed.

Every once in a while
he thinks he'll deny one—
go back where you came from.
But he likes the way they surround him
like reeds, almost identical in their formations.

In winter my mother
turns my photo to face the wall.
She told him this,
knowing he had no images,
no phone in hell.

The dead *are* mirrors:

offer them anything,
they give it back.

2. Noon

No shadow then no trapdoor
of shut eyelid no falling dream no naked dream

no friends at the field's border

they are screaming warnings

no mother alarmist on the porch
no rush no hum whisper hiss

just some music she's never heard
dark she has no proof she knows it exists

there all along in petals in pruned leaves
in the gardening books I see me I see me not

daylit moon starved for purpose all
for the taking You Can Ruin It If You Want

no shadow then only speared grass
that leaves a little singe when she steps

off earth she has to admit the idea appeals to her
there will be touch-me-nots now there will be touch-me-nots

3. Border

For years
she walks
a particular road—
the stop sign
with no one to warn,
the black blaze
of macadam,
sunflowers innumerable,
where houses once stood,
sunflowers growing
from the windshields
of junkyard cars,
struck animals.
Blooms so intensely gold
a child ignited them
with a crayon—
the road
a needle in all that gold.
She keeps pace.
Hands in pockets

disclose no trembling,
but she's not frightened,
she sees sunflowers
are breakable spines,
some lean forward
like sunstroke victims,
others lie shattered,
somewhere they have to end,
maybe just up ahead,
where the sun nosedives
and mausoleums
outline a town.

4. Venus

A bottle, dropped from a great height,
detonates at our feet. We practice agreements:
never speak again, never apologize.

We wind up in my room, where nothing is mine.
I change houses overnight, at the expense of living
things. Even the flytrap, dwarfed carnivore,

closes hungry. Maximal water,
filtered light, the old falsehoods fall short.
Capped tendrils, open exits,

from them I sliver pears to make lures.
Seduction's an adaptation, nothing less.
You don't flinch at explosions,

only the drone of my apology can draw you in.
I've changed my locks and we still wind up within.
The night passes, you are not devoured—

5. Labor Day, Circa 1980

To define *worse*, city widows brag about their brood. In their
automatic lens, it's the black sheep I most resemble.

Elder Brother lowering a Limbo baton slams it down

to keep the weakest out. Who fails to shift,

twist form to slip past. Left-back Cousin *(no hands, no hands)* carries
a rock for keepsake, chases us through the afternoon's kerosene,

later sits sucking a bone left on the grill. Sunburned Mother
hisses, we must watch for killer bees—not native, on the horizon.

How quickly we learn to say the prettiest names for fear—
Childproof, Radioactive, City Widow.

To define *emergency*: a kid's body plugged with stings.
Not one circle, not one, can outlast a line. No hands.

6. Persephone's Child

Student of the wordless,
how soon you learn not to flinch.

Shades don't remember harm.

The million hands murmur over you,
each touch an inquiry:
Are you alive

Morning brings mouths
lipsticked with recall, a river
where nothing of their lives seeps into you
when you drink from that bilge.
You are the inheritor of infinite coins
tossed from the pockets of the ferryman.

You leash the three-headed dog
and take a walk with your mother.
She tells stories of another world,
all glittering termination, all hypothesis—
trees coming into being all at once,
some never to open again.

And you consider her
following byways forbidden to others
until hands press into your shoulders like stones.

Boredom.
A synonym for *father*.

Are you alive

Next year, next year.
Earthly souvenirs she'll bring,
lurid blooms and fruit
that never hold out past the crossing.

7. Thaw

The snowless season's ending.
The yard's splintered
into a puzzle of black trees,
each black tree with its code of years.
To read them you have to
kill the trees. So the eye
divides, the heart
turns invisible, indivisible,
not one patch of garden can be seen,
rain-torn branches
nearly covering the yard.
They cover the dead birds
my mother grieves for,
hurrying to give names
like cages, while, in one
gesture, the god of spring
pickpockets all.
On his way out,
he drops the crocus,
purple coin the marl
quickly discloses.
Not an invite,
this flirtation,
crocus bruising under mud,
under felled and fractured wood—
she must lift each broken limb
to touch one
blooming mouth.

8. Rites of False Spring

How often now you call me home
before my time, mornings
waking to an alien room,
musk of earth, faint sun
on the depleted fields—ineffectual,
like light through a microwave door.
Across from the window
you stagily set the table and chair,
the jar of unremarkable blooms.
Shall I watch for blackbirds?
That's the game we used to play.
They would be starving for plunder
where the stalks froze and refused
any additional incarnations.
The old joke:
it was a dead scene, they lived on death,
everything was already taken.
I'd have to help them. I'd have to get moving.
These flowers are microphones—
they expect only sound, not meaning,
and now I feel obligated to think of something to say.
This view is blank as a blindfold
and already you're prying open
your hatches in the banks of snow—
I can't believe I'll have to fit there.

"The Books"

The poem refers to the novels *Lolita, Jane Eyre, Wide Sargasso Sea, Fahrenheit 451, 1984, To Kill a Mockingbird,* and *The Day of the Locust.*

"Decade: New York"

"I could have been somebody" was inspired by the famous lines spoken by Marlon Brando in *On the Waterfront* (dir. Elia Kazan).

"Exit Wound"

The character is based loosely on Perry Smith, one of the killers in Truman Capote's *In Cold Blood.*

Acknowledgments

Agni: "City Tree," "Lullaby"

American Letters & Commentary: "The Dare" (published as "Alias Trespass")

Cairn: "Mother," "Stranger without Candy," "The Suitors"

The Canary: "October in Idleville"

Columbia: A Journal of Literature and Art: "Labor Day, Circa 1980"

Dragonfire: "Decade: New York," "Miranda Rule"

Gulf Coast: "Thaw"

Harvard Review: "The Bridle"

Louisiana Literature: "Against Angels"

Lullwater Review: "Desert: Insomnia" (published as "Insomnia")

Mudlark: "Superstition, Inc."

Nerve: "The Lovers in the Lifeguard Chair"

The New England Review: "Do Not Duplicate"

The New York Times: "Against Angels"

The Northridge Review: "Border" (published as "A Dream of Sunflowers"), "Night Swimmer" (published as "Night Swimming")

The Olivetree Review: "Family Underworld"

ology: "The Books" (published as "Wrong Characters"); "Schiele's Trees"

The Paris Review: "Public Phone"

Ploughshares: "Exit Wound"

The St. Luke's Review: "The Chairman's Coffin" (published as "After the Avenue of Heavenly Peace")

Toronto Quarterly: "Night Stations"

West Branch: "Detour" (published as "Forget-Me-Nots")

Western Humanities Review: "Orpheus at Lethe"

The Yale Review: "Invisible Station"

I'm grateful to the faculty and staff of the Iowa Writers' Workshop, the New York University Expository Writing Program, the Bread Loaf Writers' Conference, and the James Merrill House Residency Program.

Special thanks to Marvin Bell, Oni Buchanan, Lynn Callahan, Richard Castro, Michael Collier, Marian Conroy, Steve Edles, Ben Evans, Darlene Forrest, James Galvin, Howard Gertler, Angela Glavan, Jorie Graham, Daniel Hall, Richard Howard, Pat C. Hoy II, Henry Israeli, Julia Spicher Kasdorf, Suji Kwock Kim, August Kleinzahler, David Kuhn, Timothy Liu, Silvia Marinache, J. D. McClatchy, Alice Quinn, C.J. Sage, Elizabeth Spires, Rawley Stebbens, and Susan Wheeler.

Also from The National Poetry Review Press:

Lucktown by Bryan Penberthy

Bill's Formal Complaint by Dan Kaplan

Gilgamesh at the Bellagio by Karl Elder

Legend of the Recent Past by James Haug

Urchin to Follow by Dorine Jennette

The Kissing Party by Sarah E. Barber

Deepening Groove by Ravi Shankar

The City from Nome by James Grinwis

Fort Gorgeous by Angela Vogel

Able, Baker, Charlie by John Mann

Please visit our website for more information:

www.NationalPoetryReview.com